Haunted
Histories

THE ANCIENT ORDER OF

Ghostorians

"FIAT LUX!"

(Let there be light!)

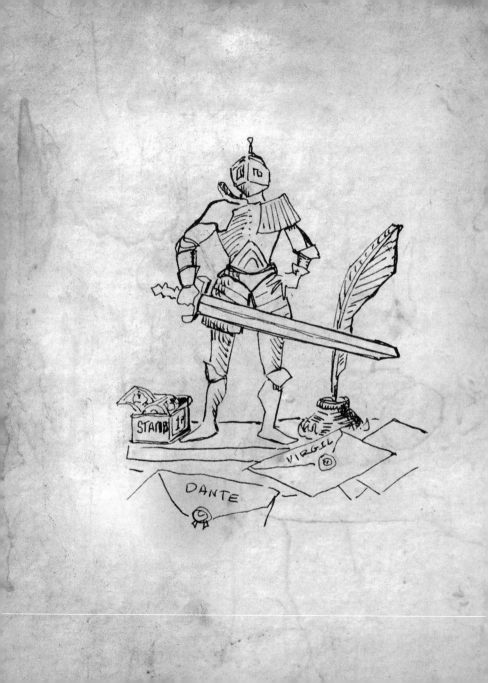

Haunted Histories

CREEPY CASTLES, DARK DUNGEONS, AND POWERFUL PALACES

J. H. Everett and
Marilyn Scott-Waters

Christy Ottaviano Books
Henry Holt and Company   NEW YORK

Henry Holt and Company, LLC
Publishers since 1866
175 Fifth Avenue
New York, New York 10010
mackids.com

Library of Congress Cataloging-in-Publication Data
Everett, J. H.
Haunted histories : creepy castles, dark dungeons, and powerful
palaces / J. H. Everett and Marilyn Scott-Waters. — 1st ed.
p. cm. — (Christy Ottaviano books)
ISBN 978-0-8050-8971-4 (hc)
1. Haunted places—Juvenile literature. 2. Ghosts—Juvenile literature.
I. Scott-Waters, Marilyn. II. Title.
BF1461.E94 2012
133.1'22—dc23
2011033495

First Edition—2012
Designed by Meredith Pratt

Printed in the United States of America by R. R. Donnelley & Sons Company,
Harrisonburg, Virginia

1 3 5 7 9 10 8 6 4 2

*To Lamar, Joe, Charles, and
the others who taught me history*
—J. H. E.

*To the Mencats, and to Jamie,
who kept us on the path.*
—M. S.-W.

Contents

GHOSTORIAN'S CREED   1

INTRODUCTION
Dying to Meet You!   3
Ghostorian 101: What Is a Ghost?   6

1: CASTLES
Real Life in Creepy Castles: Were They Pink or Did They Stink?   9
Himeji Castle   19
Krak des Chevaliers   27
The Bloody White Tower of London   33
Living Through a Siege on the Krak des Chevaliers   41
A Ghastly Ending   48

2: DUNGEONS & JAILS
Scary? Creepy? Dark? Dirty? Slimy?   51
Deadly Dungeon Design   52
Newgate Prison   56
Torment in the Tower of London   62
Castle Neuschwanstein   66

The Bastille   72

A Tortuous Life   76

Kids in Prison   81

What's in Gruel?   88

Dying to Get Out?   89

3: PALACES

Where the Powerful People Party   90

Power Plays at Hampton Court   92

Hellbrunn Water Palace—Amuse Me!   110

Jag Mandir Floating Palace   114

4: GRAVEYARDS

The Final Resting Place   118

Heraldry and the Graveyard   119

Monuments and Burial   122

The Secret Code of Heraldic Symbols   123

What Goes into a Monument?   125

HAUNTED HISTORIES TIMELINE   130

RESOURCES   135

INDEX   137

Haunted Histories

THE ANCIENT ORDER OF

GHOSTORIANS

❧ CREED ❧

WE ARE A PROFESSIONAL SOCIETY WHOSE MISSION IS TO
PROMOTE THE STUDY OF HISTORY THROUGH CONVERSATIONS
WITH GHOSTS AND THE VISITING OF HISTORICAL SITES AND
LIBRARY ARCHIVES. WE ENCOURAGE RESEARCH AND THE
SHARING OF FACTS AND IDEAS BETWEEN GHOSTORIANS
AND THE WIDER WORLD, BOTH LIVING AND DEAD, FOR
THE FURTHERANCE OF HUMANITY ON EARTH.

Let There Be Light!

My graduating class
—Virgil Dante

Introduction

Don't be frightened.

DYING TO MEET YOU!

Hello, kids. I'm Virgil Dante, a Ghostorian. What are Ghostorians? We're historians who find ghosts in the scariest, creepiest places and let them tell their own stories. I've been talking to ghosts since I was five. I'm also the youngest Master Ghostorian in London.

My job is to investigate history, often straight out of the ghost's mouth. I travel all over the world to get stories. How can a kid do all these things? I just happen to have a cursed pocket watch.

THE CURSED POCKET WATCH

The cursed pocket watch is my greatest Ghostorian tool. It's one of the oldest known pocket watches in existence. The watch buttons control time and place, and they summon ghosts so that I can talk to them. The watch also provides me a dead reckoning with a map of my current location.

I don't know when my watch gained its magical powers or even when the Ghostorians found it. The Grand High Council gave it to me for excellent performance on my spectral exams.

I never travel alone. Meet my friend who goes everywhere with me: Thor, my faithful raven scholar. He's a bit pushy. You might say that he's eaten one too many bookworms.

You are so sixteenth century!

Traveling by pocket watch ruffles my feathers.

GHOSTORIAN 101: WHAT IS A GHOST?

Let's begin with ghosts. Who are they? The playwright William Shakespeare wrote that ghosts came around to haunt the living. After certain people died, they walked the night until all the bad things they did in life were atoned for. Ghosts then returned to their graves by morning. Many people at that time believed this to be true. Some people still do. Do you?

I could use a nap.

I'm dead on my feet.

Doom'd for a certain term to walk the night,
And for the day confined to fast in fires,
Till the foul crimes done in my days of nature
Are burnt and purged away.

—*Hamlet,* act I, scene 5
WILLIAM SHAKESPEARE
English playwright *(1564–1616)*

1: Castles

REAL LIFE IN CREEPY CASTLES: WERE THEY PINK OR DID THEY STINK?

Some kids think that castles in the old days were pink and filled with princesses and ponies. Guess what? Life back then was no fairy tale. I know ghosts who can prove it. They haunt the most terrifying castles in the world: Himeji (HE-may-gee) Castle in Japan, Krak des Chevaliers (CROCK DAY she-VAHL-yay) in Syria, and the Tower of London in England. I know why people built castles. I also know how castles helped to make the world we live in today. *Let's fly!* But stick close—ghosts lurk around every dark and dripping corner. . . .

LIFE IN THE MEDIEVAL FOOD CHAIN

The medieval period lasted a long time (about the fifth to sixteenth centuries). It's the source of many ghost stories in Western Europe. People believed in a great chain of being, meaning that everyone had a particular place in the world. If you were poor, you were supposed to be poor. If you were rich, you were supposed to be rich. Many people lived poor and died young from war, disease, and lack of food. During this period, the strongest warriors battled and claimed the best land. Everyone else lived and worked to support them. Peasants lived in mud and straw houses. Kings and lords lived in heavily guarded castles because they constantly battled other lords to keep their land and power. The most powerful people liked the idea of a great chain of being because it always put them at the top!

THE MEDIEVAL "GREAT CHAIN OF BEING"

Pope   Emperor

Kings and Queens

Lords and Knights

Farmers, Craftsmen, Merchants

Peasants

People didn't want to be in the peasant class. It was dreadful.

HOW TO BUILD A CASTLE

Lords placed castles on high hills and surrounded them with deep moats. They decorated the insides with treasures and with great tapestries to keep the rooms warm in the winter. Not all castles were made of stone, as you might think. For one thing, stone was very heavy, and it took a lot of work and money to quarry and build with it. It also took a great deal of knowledge to build castles out of stone. Many lords were fine soldiers and were called knights, but had few of the skills needed to design a castle. And conquering armies simply did not have the time needed to properly build a stone castle in between attacks. So lords built their castles out of cheaper and more readily available materials, like wood, straw, and mud—not much better than the peasants' houses! Often lords had servants paint the wood to look like stone.

To scare enemies away, lords placed heads of criminals and enemies, dipped in tar, on spikes above the gates and along the road to the castle as a warning. They also displayed the bodies of condemned prisoners in gibbets, nasty iron cages hung outside the walls of the castle grounds.

Don't lose your head!

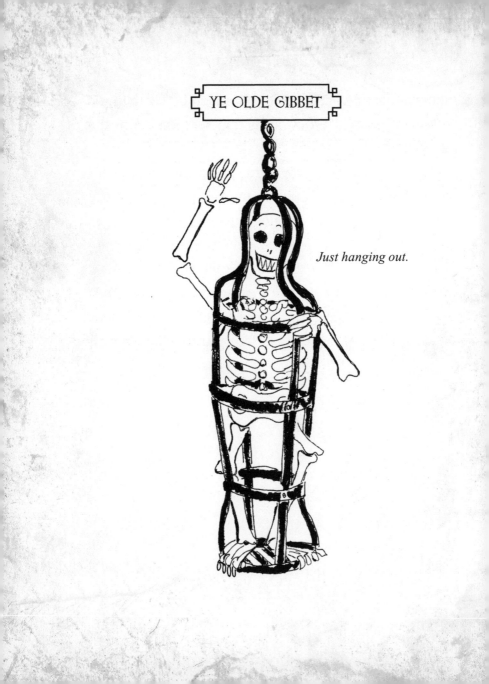

YE OLDE GIBBET

Just hanging out.

FAKE IT TILL YOU MAKE IT

How to Paint a Castle to Look Like Stone

A recipe by Thor

I. Build wooden castle walls on top of a hill.

2. Fill in holes with rocks.

3. Dig deep pits around the bottom of the hill.

4. Then dig a trench from a stream to the moat.

5. Pile dirt up around the bottom of the wall as high as possible.

6. Mix chalk and a building material called lime with water to make white paint.

7. Use plants, sap, tar, and dirt to color the paint so that the walls look like real rocks.

8. Hope that the enemies don't shoot fire arrows at the castle!

Death at the Door
THE PARTS OF A CASTLE

Before we go time traveling around the world, you should know what makes a good castle.

Allure: protected walkway on top of the interior castle wa[ll]

Bailey: a courtyard inside the walls surrounding a castle

Barbican: a gateway before the main castle gateway

Battlements: protective stone walls with cutout spaces to allow soldiers defending the castle to use weapons

Courtyard: a protected yard surrounded by walls

Curtain wall: any castle wall surrounding a courtyard

Drawbridge: a wooden bridge that can be raised and lowered over a moat to control access to a castle

Parapet

Gatehouse

Courtyard

Barbican

Battlements

Curtain wa[ll]

Drawbridge

Portcullis

Moat

Gatehouse: a building that includes the main gate of a castle

Keep: the main building of a castle

Moat: a ditch filled with water surrounding the castle walls

Parapet: the top of a protective wall

Portcullis: a wood and iron gate that can be raised and lowered to open and close a castle gateway

Postern: a small gate or door in the back side of a castle

Tower: a tall, narrow building

Now that we've got the basics of castle design and purpose, let's check out a few sinister sites and dig a little deeper. Follow me to Himeji Castle, the fortress from which the shogunate (SHOW-gun-ate) ruled the entire western region of Japan. A shogun was a powerful military leader who ruled as part of the emperor's family. Oh, and I should warn you, we'll meet a spirit there. She's usually in the foulest of moods.

Time to fly!

Himeji Castle

DING-DONG-DELL,
THERE'S SOMETHING IN THE WELL!

It may look beautiful, but Himeji Castle has a chilling history. A military fort has existed on the site since 1333, about 160 years before the European explorer Christopher Columbus arrived in the Americas. A local warlord started building a castle on this site in 1346 to protect lands from roving foot soldiers called samurai.

In 1601, a Japanese lord named Ikeda Terumasa completed the castle's construction for the Tokugawa family shogunate. Terumasa had married the shogun's daughter and distinguished himself in battle. His father-in-law sent him to Himeji in western Japan to complete the castle and to subdue the local warlords, bringing them under Tokugawa's control.

Himeji Castle
THE DEADLY BEAUTY OF JAPAN

LEVEL 4

Moat 2

Moats to tire out the enemy

Secret passages to position for counterattack

LEVEL 2

Moat 1

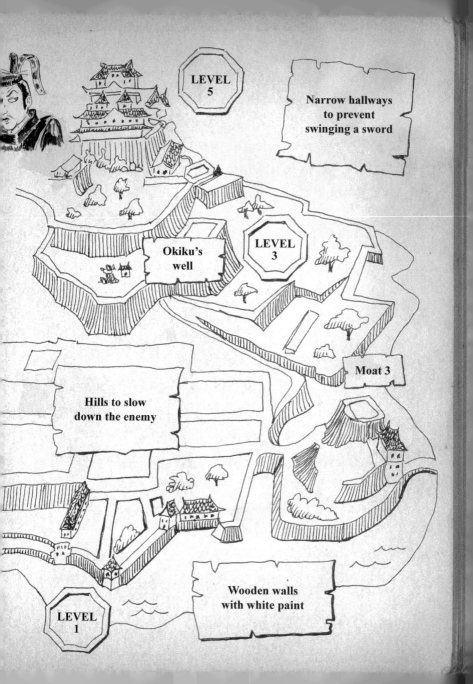

LEVEL
5

Narrow hallways
to prevent
swinging a sword

LEVEL
3

Okiku's
well

Moat 3

Hills to slow
down the enemy

Wooden walls
with white paint

LEVEL
1

Tokugawa gave Terumasa 3 million bushels of rice to pay for the completion of Himeji Castle.

Himeji was five levels high, built on a hill, with three moats. Each moat was more difficult to cross than the last. The hill and moats were designed to slow down and tire out enemy soldiers. The halls were like mazes meant to confuse enemies who got inside the buildings. Narrow stairwells and corridors prevented soldiers from swinging swords. This beautiful castle was never successfully attacked. It was the perfect castle to control and expand landholdings for Tokugawa.

Himeji Castle's most famous ghost is the spirit of fourteen-year-old Okiku. She is known as a *yuurei*, a traditional Japanese female ghost who seeks revenge for the wrongs done to her. These ghosts, known for their screaming, are particularly unpleasant to meet. Her specter now rests in the bottom of the castle's bloody well. . . .

OKIKU IS IN THE WELL

Okiku was not always a hideous spirit of the dead. In life, she was a servant for the lord of Himeji Castle.

Her job was to protect ten precious golden plates. When she warned the lord that assassins were plotting to kill him, he imprisoned them.

But then, one of the jailed assassins escaped and sought revenge on Okiku. He stole one of the golden plates and convinced the lord that Okiku was guilty of the crime. The lord became very angry and threw her into the well, where she died. Every day, before dawn, Okiku howls and counts the plates. . . .

One, two, three, four, five, six, seven, eight, nine . . . AAAHHHHHHHHhhhhh!

Because of the drama surrounding her death, Okiku's story is a favorite subject for Japanese popular theater, Kabuki. Kabuki theater originated in the poorest areas of Japan in the early 1600s. But soon after it started, everyone from the poorest to the richest loved it.

The stories were on forbidden subjects like revenge, murder, and love.

Only men were allowed onstage to perform both male and female roles!

Kabuki theater brought together all the different social classes of Japan. Just as in Western Europe, the Japanese feudal system placed people into different levels of power and wealth. These different classes almost never talked to each other, except at the theater. And now, in the grave. . . .

Lords built castles to control land. They operated

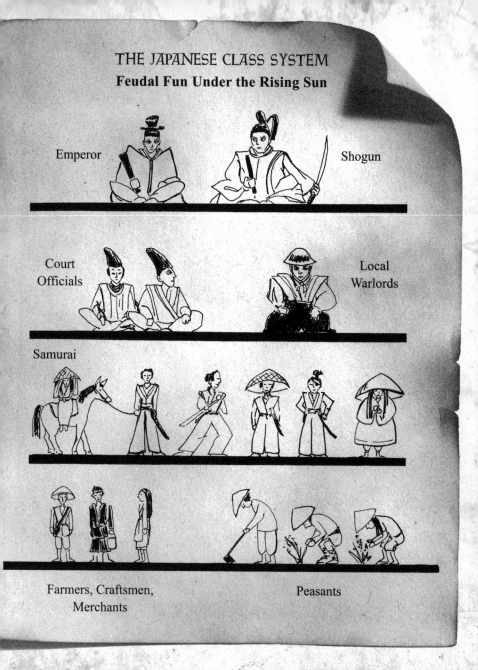

THE JAPANESE CLASS SYSTEM
Feudal Fun Under the Rising Sun

Emperor

Shogun

Court
Officials

Local
Warlords

Samurai

Farmers, Craftsmen,
Merchants

Peasants

courts and government from the castles, and used them to impress foreign enemies. But a castle's main job was to protect the people living in it against attack. And even though a castle could be made of anything, strong stone walls always worked the best.

So where are the most awesome examples of the biggest castle walls that were meant to repel an enemy attack? Take a guess! Hint—they're not in England. And not in Germany or France. In fact, some of the strongest castle walls are in Syria, in the Middle East. Are you ready for another quick trip? Hang on to your hoodies!

Time to fly!

Krak des Chevaliers

DIGGING UP THE TOUGHEST PLACE IN TOWN

Ah, the Krak des Chevaliers, meaning the fortress of the knights. This castle has stood since 1031. From the surrounding plain it is 2,300 feet tall and guards the only pass between Turkey and Lebanon. It once housed more than 4,000 soldiers. During the Crusades (Western European invasion of the Middle East) in 1142, an order of knights from Europe, known as the Hospitallers, took over the castle and expanded it. The knights in the Krak held back at least twelve major sieges. How did they pull it off? Let's ask the spirits of the warriors who occupied it.

The outer wall defenses of the Krak des Chevaliers are among the best in the world. Even with the best

In 1099, Fulk of Chartres, a Crusader knight, had this to say about the Krak des Chevaliers:

"The lower half of the wall is solid masonry, of square stones and mortar, sealed with molten lead. So strong is this wall that, if fifteen or twenty men should be well supplied with provisions, they would never be taken by any army."

siege technology and highly skilled armies, it was almost impossible to fight this castle and win.

But in the end, the Krak's amazing defenses really didn't matter. In 1271, the Mamluk, who were slave soldiers, attacked the Krak for more than a month. Sultan Baibars, their leader, then figured out a sneaky way to get inside. He forged a letter to the knights in the castle from their leader, the Grand Master of the Knights Hospitaller, who was in Tripoli. The fake letter said that the Grand Master had negotiated with the sultan to grant the knights safe passage home to Europe. All the knights had to do was to give up the castle and go to Tripoli. Even though the Krak's people had enough supplies to survive a year-long siege, they grew tired of the constant bombardment from Baibars's war machines. They packed up and left. Baibars gave them no trouble as they went.

Then he sent in the Mamluk to take over the empty castle.

Pretty clever, huh?

Go home! Love, Your Boss

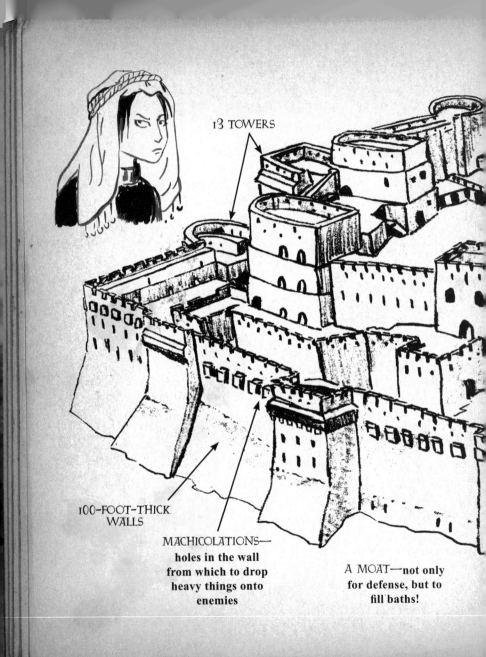

13 TOWERS

100-FOOT-THICK
WALLS

MACHICOLATIONS—
holes in the wall
from which to drop
heavy things onto
enemies

A MOAT—not only
for defense, but to
fill baths!

Krak des Chevaliers
THIRTEEN TOWERS OF SHEER TERROR

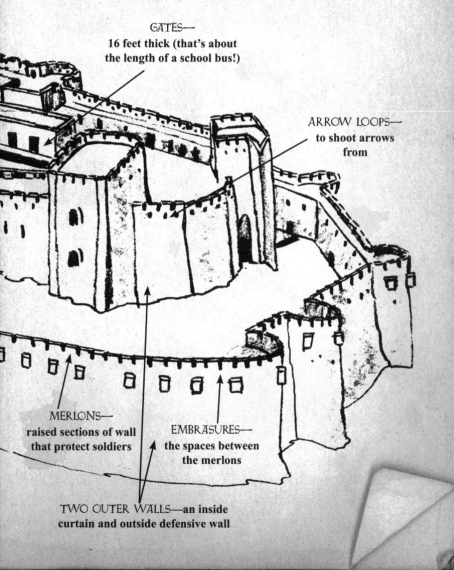

GATES—
**16 feet thick (that's about
the length of a school bus!)**

ARROW LOOPS—
**to shoot arrows
from**

MERLONS—
**raised sections of wall
that protect soldiers**

EMBRASURES—
**the spaces between
the merlons**

TWO OUTER WALLS—**an inside
curtain and outside defensive wall**

*I love a nice moldy castle—
more worms for me!*

Now that we've broken through the mysteries of the outside of a castle, it's time to find out if it was really any better to live on the inside of one. I assure you, living in a castle was not all silk mattresses and unicorn tapestries. In fact, castle life was absolutely disgusting. Ready to return to England? Here we go!

The Bloody White Tower of London

ROLL OUT THE DEAD CARPET!

The White Tower, at the Tower of London, is a lodestone keep—the central tower of a castle. William the Conqueror originally had his builders construct it out of wood in 1078 to claim Britain as his own and to control rowdy Londoners. Later, William and his successors decided to make the Tower the strongest fortress they could, so they expanded it by adding stone walls. Because London was the most important city in Britain, the Tower became the most important castle.

Castles were military strongholds built for war. But

kings also lived and worked in them. Earl William fitz Osbourne is thought to be one of the men who helped design the White Tower and many other castles for King William I. The king made fitz Osbourne an earl in 1067, giving him one of the first aristocratic titles in England.

William I conquered the British Isles in 1066. The earl helped him build castles wherever he won battles.

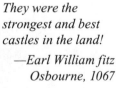

They were the strongest and best castles in the land!
—*Earl William fitz Osbourne, 1067*

What did castles look like on the inside? Pretty unpleasant. The king designed the White Tower to have the best that the world had to offer in the eleventh century (everything a lord could desire). Loads of explosives and weapons, smoke-filled rooms, a place to hang hunted meat, a dungeon, and even indoor toilets . . . sort of.

And I want to add a toilet and some sea serpents.

Yes, your majesty.

Nasty Business
LIVING AT THE WHITE TOWER

1. ***Gotta go?*** Tower residents called the bathroom a "garderobe." It was a stone seat with a hole in the middle. Waste ran right down the outside of the castle wall.

2. ***You smell what?*** Servants and workers in the castle took baths only a couple of times a year and often had just one set of clothes for most of their lives.

3. ***Don't swim in it!*** People dumped all their garbage and waste, including animal guts, in the moat.

4. ***Are you hungry?*** Salted meats (dead animals) hung in all the kitchen areas.

5. ***Are you comfy?*** If you were a servant, you lay on the floor or leaned up against a wall to sleep.

6. ***Sweet dreams!*** If you did get to sleep in a bed, it was probably infested with bedbugs.

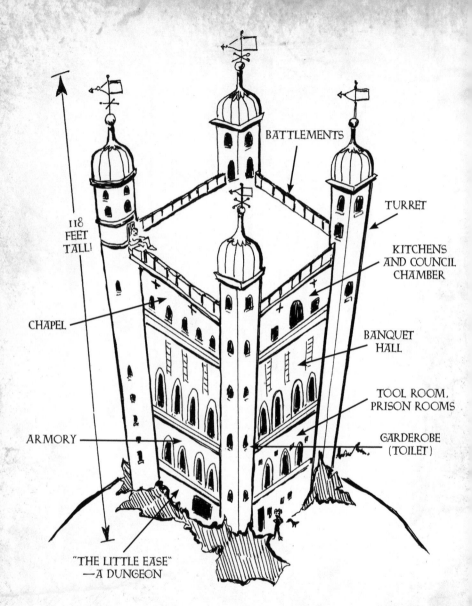

118
FEET
TALL!

BATTLEMENTS

TURRET

KITCHENS
AND COUNCIL
CHAMBER

CHAPEL

BANQUET
HALL

TOOL ROOM,
PRISON ROOMS

ARMORY

GARDEROBE
(TOILET)

"THE LITTLE EASE"
—A DUNGEON

The greasy, grimy guts of the White Tower of London

Here are the ghosts of two young princes in the Tower: Edward V, age 13, and his brother, Richard, Duke of York, age 10. Edward was the crown prince at the time of their disappearance. It is said that they still haunt the Bloody Tower today. And, even though they are often seen playing and laughing around the castle grounds, their last days at the Tower were less than happy.

Noogies in the 15th century!

Come and play with us.

Edward was supposed to become king of England in 1483. Instead, his uncle Richard captured the boys and held them prisoner. Soon after, they both disappeared.

Many people said that their uncle (who became King Richard III) killed them. Other people think that Edward died and Richard escaped. The Tower may have kept many kings safe, but these two young princes learned that it could be murder to live there.

The keep and other buildings in a castle helped to protect the families of the lords, their armies, and their servants. They also provided a place for business and politics. But the rooms weren't comfortable by today's standards. Garbage, waste, bug bites—how dreadful! And what happened when things got really hard for people living in castles, such as when a castle was under attack? Let's zoom back to Syria to find out. . . .

Living Through a Siege of the Krak des Chevaliers

A FRIGHT TO THE DEATH

Welcome to the year 1271, just outside the siege camp of Sultan Baibars. He is about to attack the Krak des Chevaliers. Things look serious. Women and children are filling clay pots with flammable goo and sharpening giant arrows.

Slave kids and adults are walking in giant war machines. Men and horses ride siege towers right up to the castle to help their soldiers get over the walls. The defending knights in the castle are busy loading spears into springalds, giant crossbows on the top of the towers. They are also heating up giant pots of oil. The fight is about to begin.

Six of One to Win!

TIPS FOR ATTACKING A CASTLE

✤ Dig a trench under the walls and light the walls on fire.

✤ Poison the castle's wells and cut off the drinking water.

✤ Launch fire pots and fire arrows into the castle.

✤ Build big machines like siege towers (wooden towers to lift soldiers over the wall), mangonels (machines to hurl big stones), and trebuchets (giant slingshots) to smash through castle defenses.

✤ Build a battering ram to crash through the front gates.

✤ Use germ warfare— toss diseased dead animals over the wall.

Half a Dozen to Die . . .

TIPS FOR DEFENDING A CASTLE

- ✠ Light animal fat on fire at the base of the castle walls, so that enemies can't dig their way in.
- ✠ Make sure that there is enough food and supplies for several months.
- ✠ If the water supply is cut off, get ready to drink urine.
- ✠ Build catapult machines and springalds on top of the walls and towers.
- ✠ Train lots of archers to shoot arrows at enemies. Position them for attack.
- ✠ Train children to use slingshots to hurl rocks at the enemy. Every little rock helps!

Revolting Jobs for Kids in a War

+ Walk inside wheels to move giant machines.
+ Help stir pots of boiling goo made of tar, sap, and alcohol.
+ Taunt enemy knights, because you can . . . "Sissy!"
+ Carry supplies for soldiers.
+ Find rocks to throw at enemies.
+ Help sew clothing for soldiers.
+ Help raise and clean up after animals.
+ Collect food for soldiers.
+ Crawl inside small spaces to check for cracks in the walls.
+ Stoke fires day and night.

Little Barbarians!

Sissies!

So, what did the richest kids do in war? They trained to be knights, lords, and ladies like their parents. The lord and lady of the house encouraged their children to become defenders of the family lands and wealth. Many of them didn't think much of school.

The Ostrogoths, also known as the Goths, were an empire of barbarians (according to the Romans) from the area that is now Germany. By the sixth century, they had a kingdom of their own. Procopius was a famous historian who recorded the history of the Goths. Queen Amalasuntha was a Goth queen. Here is what they said about school.

"School is unmanly and turns kids into sissies."
      —Procopius, quoting the Ostrogoths, circa 520 C.E.

"Your father would never allow any of the Goths to send their children to school."
      —Queen Amalasuntha, circa 520 C.E.

It may sound fun to miss school, but the Goths figured a child was better off getting his head smashed in instead of reading books!

One of the things kids got to do in war was to hurl insults at the enemies. The Goths were famous for their insults during battle. Historians have learned that many of their insults are still used today. The Goths actually called people sissies! Just as it means today, the word meant that someone was weak and unmanly.

So castles are all about power?

It's always about power.

A GHASTLY ENDING

Castles were all about war and controlling territory. They helped kings and lords hold the land that they won in battles and gave them somewhere safe to live while they fought to gain more land and more power. As we have seen, most castles were not known for their comfort.

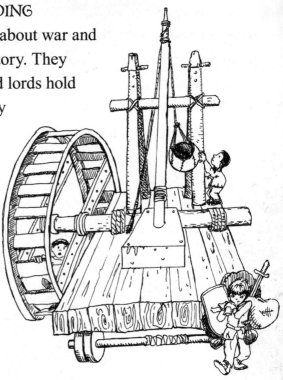

Castles helped to define the borders of a lord's land, and eventually strings of castles defined entire kingdoms. Over time, those kingdoms became the countries and states that we know today.

In battles, armies cap-
tured enemies, and those
prisoners needed to be put
somewhere. How better
to deal with enemies than
a wickedly gloomy, fear-
inspiring dungeon? I warn
you—spirits who died in
dungeons are particularly
nasty. Step lively, now. . . .

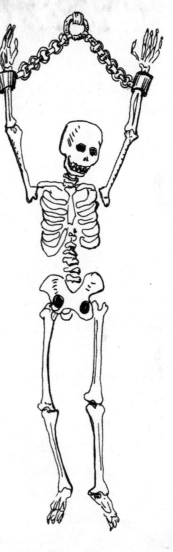

BEWARE THE COIN OF THE REALM . . .

Another way kings defined the borders of their lands was by minting coins with their portraits pressed into them. As the coins were used for trade, they often traveled far and extended a king's power well beyond his original territory.

"I am the state."
— King Louis XIV of France
(1643–1715)

Oooh, shiny!

2: Dungeons & Jails

SCARY? CREEPY? DARK? DIRTY? SLIMY?
DYING TO GET BEHIND THE IRON BARS

Have you seen creepy dungeons and old jails in movies? They are actually scarier in real life! The ghosts that haunt such dark and dank places are a nasty lot. Ghosts haunt infamous places like the Tower of London and Newgate Prison in England, the theatrical Neuschwanstein dungeon in Bavaria, and the area of the terrifying Bastille prison in France.

Originally, in ancient Europe and Asia, kings and their architects built dungeons and jails high up in the towers of castles and in fortified city gate buildings, so that the rulers could keep a close eye on their prisoners. However, most rulers did not like the groans, screams, and stink coming from the dungeons, so they moved them out of their houses to new buildings, but not too far. Dungeons and jails let rulers control their lands through fear and pain. Prisons were filled with people who owed money, everyday criminals, and military enemies—anyone who threatened the king's power and wealth. Let's meet some of these dungeon dwellers. . . .

DEADLY DUNGEON DESIGN
WHERE EVERYTHING BAD IS GOOD!
The word *dungeon* comes from the French *donjon*, which means "tower." So how did they end up as dark holes in the ground? After the first Crusades in the late eleventh century, Europeans copied the underground dungeons that they saw in the Middle East. Because of

the extreme temperature changes between the heat of day and cold of night in the middle of the desert, jails in towers could kill a prisoner very quickly. Rulers of these desert lands built jails underground as an act of mercy to help keep prisoners alive. But European knights who had gone on the Crusades learned that underground prisons could also be dark and scary—a useful tactic for controlling enemies. Back in Europe, one of the worst things about a dungeon was exposure to cold, snow, and flooding from nearby rivers. Each night, the tides rose in the River Thames and flooded the floors of the dungeon, drowning or half drowning the people inside. Prisoners were not just miserable and hungry, they had to withstand bad weather, rats, bugs, and disease, as well as torture. This made them much weaker and easier to control.

The Dungeon Rogues Gallery

These characters knew no mercy. To them, there was no such thing as reform of a criminal. They believed that no matter how small, all crimes should be severely punished.

SHERIFF

the main officer in charge of law and peacekeeping in a specific region, usually a town

JUDGE

any person who had the right to hear cases in a court of law

GAOLER (JAILER)

the officer in charge of the administration and running of a jail and daily care of prisoners

GUARD

any person, often an armed soldier or a man with military experience, who watched over jails and prisoners on a daily basis

EXECUTIONER

the person hired by justice officials to carry out the sentence when people were found guilty of crimes worth the death penalty

Newgate Prison

LONDON'S LIMBO FOR THE UNLUCKY

Newgate Prison in London was one of the most notorious prisons ever built. The prison was constructed in the late twelfth century out of one of the two original gates of London on an execution site created by the Romans around 200 C.E. Most often, judges put people into jail for owing money or refusing to appear in court. Often people refused to go to court in London because it was very expensive for them. They had to pay for their trip to London, no matter where they lived in the kingdom, and they had to pay all the fees and costs associated with the trial—even if they won their case! Once arrested and put in jail, they had to stay until they agreed to go to court, until their family paid for them to get out, or until they died from the cold, starvation, or one of the many contagious diseases in the prison.

"I was outside Newgate. . . . Two young ladies walked round me, within a few yards of the ground reserved for the scaffold; and the worst class of boys and ruffians in London were already taking their places. The rest of the scene was like a diabolical fair."

—*Charles Dickens, 1864*
English author and activist

As in the Tower of London and other dungeons and jails, prisoners could have family members and servants stay with them in prison if they wanted to. But it cost a lot. Prisoners had to pay for every little thing. For instance, they had to pay to get into jail, for their chains, for their food and drink, for their bed, and eventually to get out of jail. The poorer a prisoner was, the worse the experience in jail. Many rich noble people lived in relatively fancy jail cells, enjoying all the comforts of their normal lives—except their freedom.

Newgate held 50 to 100 prisoners at any given time, but an amazing number of prisoners didn't stay very long because they were executed. The front of the prison was black from the smoke of burnings at the stake. Up to the eighteenth century, more than 350 different crimes, everything from stealing bread to murder, could carry the death penalty. Here's an idea of how the jails and prisons were organized:

CELLS • 20 to 30 cells held one or two prisoners each. Dimensions: 8 or 9 feet tall by about 8 feet long and 6 feet wide. Each cell contained a bench, a rug, and a prayer book. An iron candlestick hung on the wall, and a small window was near the top of the cell with a double row of heavy iron bars and no glass or shutters.

DEBTORS' EXERCISE YARD

DEBTORS' PRISON for people who owed money

WARDS • 12 to 14 common rooms. Large, high-ceilinged rooms could hold several people at once. No water, no bathroom. Corpses were left in the corners to rot until their families could pay to get the bodies out of prison.

TURNKEY ROOMS • For wealthier prisoners who could pay for privileges, including the freedom to go to work and to have family visitors. But they had to return to jail every night.

Newgate Prison
ONE OF THE DARKEST PRISONS IN ENGLAND

Most prisoners died long before their execution date. If they stayed silent and would not consent to go to court, they were pressed to death with heavy weights on their chests. Or they starved to death. Or they died of one of many different prison diseases, such as typhus (called "jail fever").

MEN'S PRISON
AND EXERCISE YARD

WOMEN'S PRISON
AND EXERCISE YARD

pel

THE KNOCKER ON THE FRONT
DOOR WAS VERY FAMOUS. It was
so black from burnings at the stake
that it became common to say some-
thing was "as black as the knocker
of Newgate Prison."

Torment in the Tower of London

YOU GET WHAT YOU PAY FOR: PRISON CELL LIVING IN THE 16TH CENTURY

A wealthy or royal prisoner in the Tower of London could be kept in a well-furnished cell with servants, family members, and even pets. Or a cell might be a living nightmare, with a torture chamber, rats, and straw-covered stone floors that flooded at high tide. Some dungeons, like those located in and around the Tower of London, also had special cells that were designed to torture. Some were so small and narrow that a prisoner had to stand in a skinny, little space all day and night. Other cells had holes in the floor where prisoners were forced to sit curled up in a ball.

Many prisoners scratched at the stone walls to keep their minds busy during their stay in prison. Let's look at messages and graffiti that they left behind.

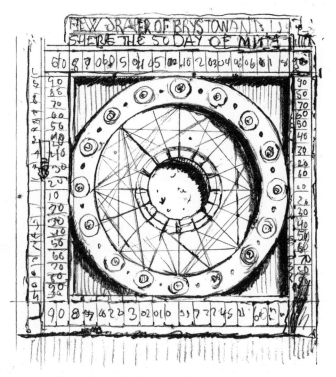

*Hugh Draper's Bizarre Astronomical Clock
in the Salt Tower (1561)*

Carved in Stone

FAMOUS PRISONERS OF THE TOWER
WHO LEFT THEIR MARK ON A WALL

SIR WALTER RALEIGH

supposedly Queen
Elizabeth's boyfriend
(1605–1618; executed)

ROBERT DUDLEY,
EARL OF LEICESTER

Queen Elizabeth's
other boyfriend
(released in 1554)

ARUNDELL

PHILIP HOWARD, EARL OF ARUNDEL

got caught cheering for the Catholic side in Protestant England
(1585–1595; died in prison)

JANE

LADY JANE GREY

the Queen's cousin, and queen herself for nine days
(executed in 1554)

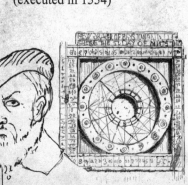

HUGH DRAPER

So smart he got accused of being a wizard
(1561; unknown demise)

1845-1886

Castle Neuschwanstein

LET'S PLAY DUNGEON: HOW TO SCARE
FRIENDS AND INFLUENCE PEOPLE

In 1869, crazy King Ludwig II of Bavaria (1845–1886) started building his castle, Neuschwanstein.

Ludwig was also called "the Cloud King" and "the Fairy Tale King."

I bet they didn't call him that to his face.

"LET THE TRAITORS BE THROWN
INTO THE DEEPEST DUNGEON,
LOADED WITH CHAINS, AND LEAVE
THEM TO DIE OF STARVATION."
—*Ludwig II, King of Bavaria, 1886*

In reality, Ludwig's dungeon was nothing more than a cellar pretending to be a dungeon with fake, scary lighting and theatrical paint.

Ludwig was a very shy, creative person. He loved music and was the main patron of a famous composer named Richard Wagner. Much of Ludwig's early life was spent in the city of Munich, but Ludwig didn't like the big city. It was often said that he didn't really like the people in Munich. He would arrange unusual events, such as orchestra concerts and operas in the largest performance halls for himself and absolutely no one else.

Ludwig preferred to be in the countryside, surrounded by his favorite birds—swans. (Ludwig was also called "the Swan King." He probably didn't mind that so much.) He believed in the purity of nature and wanted to be closer to it than he could be in the city. The problem was that Ludwig seemed to be mentally

"An eternal mystery will I remain to myself and others!"

—*Ludwig II, King of Bavaria, 1876*

unstable; mental illness plagued his family. He used an enormous amount of his wealth to build castles and to throw huge parties at a time when the people of his kingdom were very poor. But many of the poorest people defended him anyway and didn't think him crazy at all.

Ludwig made Castle Neuschwanstein so elegant that even today it is depicted in many fairy tales and picture books. For Ludwig, it was important that everything look perfect, like a theater show. So he made his dungeon appear scary by using theater paint and props, even special colored lights, to give it the full effect. Ludwig used his fake dungeon for parties more than torture. Like almost everything else in his life, it was just for show.

Though we don't know for sure, it is believed that Ludwig went completely insane. He and his private doctor were found dead in the lake near one of his other castles, called Castle Berg. To this day, no one knows whether he killed himself or was murdered for political reasons. Ludwig's brother, Otto, became king after he died, and things didn't get any better. Ludwig's sad ghost is said to still wander both of his castles and the shallows of Lake Starnberg, where he died.

So it was all fake?

MADE BY LUDWIG

For the most part, yes.

The Bastille

PRISON FOR THE POSH
WITH A FRENCH FLAIR

The Bastille was originally constructed starting in 1370 as a fortress during a conflict between the French and English called the Hundred Years' War. It was built in Paris in the middle of swampland. In the seventeenth century, the French king's powerful first minister, Cardinal Richelieu, converted the fortress into a prison for the wealthiest people in the kingdom. Most often these were political prisoners, rebellious writers, and people whose families requested their imprisonment for embarrassing the family, insanity, or owing money. Many of the prisoners in the Bastille were arrested by *lettres de cachet* (letters signed by the king). The king imprisoned anyone he wanted to at any time. He might do it because they were in debt or because they had said things that the king didn't like. It was all quite arbitrary.

Many of the Bastille's wealthy prisoners served their time with all the comforts and luxuries that they could afford. Nevertheless, it was the Bastille's cold, stone floors and dark towers that struck fear in people. Its reputation was one of brutality and isolation— everything that the French people hated about the kings of France. In 1789, as one of the first dramatic acts in the French Revolution, the people completely destroyed the prison in a famous attack called "the Storming of the Bastille."

I will not talk about the King.

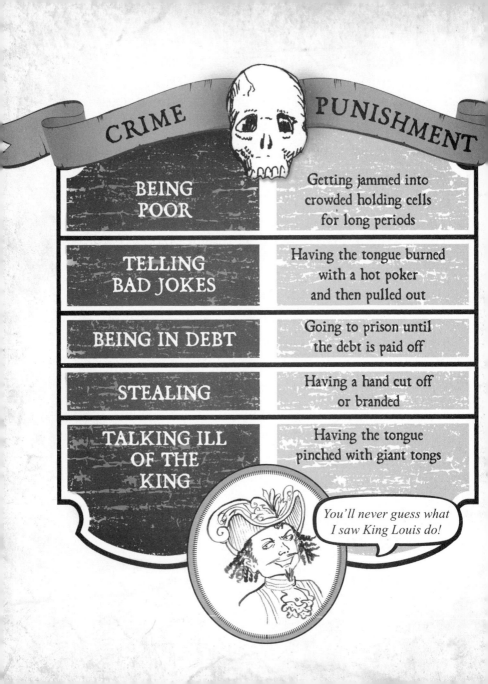

CRIME	PUNISHMENT
BEING POOR	Getting jammed into crowded holding cells for long periods
TELLING BAD JOKES	Having the tongue burned with a hot poker and then pulled out
BEING IN DEBT	Going to prison until the debt is paid off
STEALING	Having a hand cut off or branded
TALKING ILL OF THE KING	Having the tongue pinched with giant tongs

You'll never guess what I saw King Louis do!

A Torturous Life
TOP TEN TORTURE DEVICES

Jailers designed most torture devices to look terrifying. In fact, just showing a torture device to prisoners was usually enough to get a confession out of them.

THE RACK
a scary machine that stretched
people like a piece of taffy

THUMBSCREWS
small finger-crushing machines
that caused excruciating pain

IRON MAIDEN
a gory cabinet filled with sharp spikes used to turn prisoners into Swiss cheese

SHACKLES
heavy iron cuffs placed over the wrists or ankles, used to hold prisoners in place or keep them from moving too fast

GIBBET
a human birdcage hanging
from a beam that exposed
people to the weather

MINISTER'S CHAIR
a spiked chair that worked a lot
like the iron maiden, only out in
the open so that the torturer
could ask questions and watch
a prisoner suffer

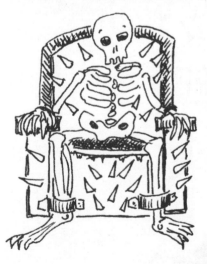

SCAVENGER'S DAUGHTER

an iron clamp and bar
that held the body in a
bent-over position for
long periods of time

IMPRESSMENT

placing a plank and heavy stones on a prisoner's
chest; torturers added stones, "pressing" the
prisoner until the person could no longer breathe;
used to get people to agree to go to court

ISOLATION

placing prisoners in small, dark spots, away from all other prisoners and in one position for days, weeks, or months

SCOLD'S BRIDE

a metal mask to publicly embarrass prisoners. It had a metal strip that went into the mouth and held the tongue down, preventing the prisoner from speaking, gossiping, or nagging

HA

HA HA

Kids in Prison
AND YOU THOUGHT SCHOOL WAS BAD!

Kids were not left out of dungeons or punishment. Special prisons called workhouses were designed for the poor; many were specifically built to house kids. Workhouses were often a combination of an orphanage and a jail where kids were made to work for nine to ten hours a day to earn their food and bed. The hours were brutal, and the work was grueling. Kids lived and slept together in large, open rooms. They died from diseases caused by the filthy surroundings and starvation. The adults who created these places actually thought they were being nice!

Daily Workhouse Activities for Kids
NO FUN HERE! HORRIBLE CHORES AND BUSYWORK

Picking apart rough sea ropes to make oakum to sell at the market. Oakum was used to make new ropes, repair walls, and fix boats.

Digging holes and refilling them to keep kids from causing trouble and to tire them out. Doing nothing was considered evil.

Crushing animal bones to make things like glue.

Milling grain to make bread.

Breaking and moving stone for no particular reason.

Cutting and stacking wood to heat the workhouse.

Doing needlework to make clothing or draperies, and to earn money for the workhouse.

Washing and scrubbing around the workhouse.

"AS REGARDS MALES, FOR EACH ENTIRE DAY
OF DETENTION—THE BREAKING OF . . . STONES
OR THE PICKING OF FOUR POUNDS OF UNBEATEN
OR EIGHT POUNDS OF BEATEN OAKUM; OR NINE
HOURS' WORK IN DIGGING OR PUMPING, OR
CUTTING WOOD, OR GRINDING CORN.

AS REGARDS FEMALES, FOR EACH ENTIRE
DAY OF DETENTION—THE PICKING OF TWO
POUNDS OF UNBEATEN OR FOUR POUNDS OF
BEATEN OAKUM; OR NINE HOURS' WORK IN
WASHING, SCRUBBING, AND CLEANING, OR
NEEDLEWORK."

—J. D. Dodson, president,
Departmental Committee on Vagrancy, 1882

Discipline was very strict in the workhouses. Even though punishments were enforced, fights still broke out. Fighting most often erupted . . . in the girls' yards!

You fight like a boy!

Take that back!

The Daily Menu

THE CRUEL SCHOOL
OF DAILY GRUEL

6 to 8 ounces of bread

1 pint of gruel

1 pint of broth

1 ounce of cheese

That's it for the day!

Gruel is the pits.

What's in Gruel?

THE SECRET INGREDIENT IS . . . WATER

In Charles Dickens's stories, Oliver Twist, Bob Cratchit, and Old Scrooge himself all ate it. But what's in it?

Gruel is a disgusting, watery version of porridge (sort of like oatmeal) made with lots of hot water and whatever grain is available, including rye, oats, and wheat. In many lists from nineteenth-century workhouses, it was written that the best gruel was almost all water because that saved money.

DYING TO GET OUT?

If dungeons and work-houses were so effective in intimidating people, why might a king want to treat a potential enemy with dignity? Why would he throw an enemy a big,  fancy-dress party with the finest food, clothing, and art in the land? Well, for starters, it certainly made a bloodthirsty ruler look a little nicer to the people he ruled. Kings liked to look good, even if they were bad. Sometimes it was a great advantage to keep enemies close in order to control them or watch them.

I'll take a party any day!

3: Palaces

WHERE THE POWERFUL PEOPLE PARTY

Palace ghosts tend to be the friendliest on a ghost scale, and they haunt some of the most expensive and beautiful buildings ever built, such as Hampton Court Palace just outside of London, England; Hellbrunn Water Palace in Salzburg, Austria; and the amazing Jag Mandir Floating Palace in Udaipur, India. Like castles, palaces still served as protection, but that was not their main purpose. Palaces were more open and inviting. They were made to show off the wealth of their royal owners. In place of the turrets with big weapons and the giant stone walls of castles, palaces had frilly towers, giant walking gardens, courtyards with water fountains, and inviting driveways where famous guests could pull up and be seen by people when they arrived. Palaces were built for giving dignitaries the red-carpet treatment on their way in to giant parties. The real heart of any palace was the kitchen and dining rooms. Time to meet some glamorous celebrity ghosts. *Let's fly!*

Power Plays at Hampton Court

TOO MUCH OF A GOOD THING CAN BE WONDERFUL!

It may seem like living in a palace was all about pleasure, but that's not the case. Sure, a palace was more comfortable than a military-oriented castle, but it still had a job to do. A palace let people know how powerful kings and queens were, but in a more pleasant way than locking people in dungeons. Royalty would throw fancy parties and giant banquets to welcome rulers from other kingdoms and show them just how fabulous, rich, and in control their hosts were.

Because the king or queen ran the government, their home was the center of all politics and business within a kingdom.

Take Hampton Court—packed with ghosts, including King Henry VIII and several of his six wives, Anne Boleyn, Jane Seymour, and Catherine Howard.

Many of his wives found him to be a real pain in the neck. It is said that several famous wives of Henry VIII haunt Hampton Court to this day.

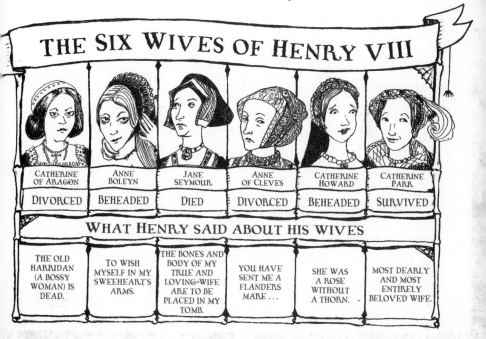

THE SIX WIVES OF HENRY VIII

CATHERINE OF ARAGON	ANNE BOLEYN	JANE SEYMOUR	ANNE OF CLEVES	CATHERINE HOWARD	CATHERINE PARR
DIVORCED	BEHEADED	DIED	DIVORCED	BEHEADED	SURVIVED

WHAT HENRY SAID ABOUT HIS WIVES

| THE OLD HARRIDAN (A BOSSY WOMAN) IS DEAD. | TO WISH MYSELF IN MY SWEEHEART'S ARMS. | THE BONES AND BODY OF MY TRUE AND LOVING-WIFE ARE TO BE PLACED IN MY TOMB. | YOU HAVE SENT ME A FLANDERS MARE ... | SHE WAS A ROSE WITHOUT A THORN. - | MOST DEARLY AND MOST ENTIRELY BELOVED WIFE. |

And here comes His Majesty King Henry VIII now, with the ghost of his first wife, Catherine of Aragon. When they first married, they were the happiest of couples. But they didn't stay that way.

King Henry VIII ruled England from 1491 to 1547. But he was never meant to be king at all. His father, Henry VII, won the right to be king by defeating King Richard III at the Battle of Bosworth Field. Henry became king only after his brother Arthur (named after the legendary King Arthur) died, leaving him next in line for the throne.

The people of England considered Henry VIII to be a very handsome man. He played sports and liked to hunt. Many thought he was a good king. However, his subjects didn't want to get on his bad side. According to the records of the time, there were some 72,000 executions during his reign.

Henry married six times because he wanted a son to take over his throne. He finally had a son named Edward with Jane Seymour, but she died shortly after giving birth. When Henry died, in 1547, his son was crowned Edward VI of England at the age of nine. Edward was always very sick, and he reigned for only six years. Henry also had two daughters, Mary (with Catherine of Aragon) and Elizabeth (with Anne Boleyn), who grew to become powerful queens.

Sisters...

Hello, Elizabeth.

Hello, Mary.

Hampton Court Palace
A PALACE FIT FOR A KING (SO HE TOOK IT!)

Hampton Court was built by Thomas Wolsey. He was the Lord Chancellor of England—second in command under King Henry VIII and very rich. Wolsey assembled the palace out of a smaller set of manor-house buildings that had been standing for hundreds of years. By the time he was finished renovating, the palace was gigantic. It had more than 300 rooms and needed a staff of about 5,000 to run it. It was the grandest palace in Europe, and Cardinal Wolsey knew it.

THE CARDINAL SPIDER
**Hairy and Scary—
Even Scarier Than
the Cardinal Himself**

One of the creepy
things that you can see
at Hampton Court Palace today is a
spider with huge, hairy legs named after
Cardinal Wolsey: the Cardinal Spider
(*Tegenaria parietina*). It can grow up to
three and a half inches, about the size
of a regular doughnut, and is a common night-
crawling spider that lives around southern
England. Though these spiders terrified their
namesake, Cardinal Wolsey, they were thought
to bring good luck to the kings and queens of
England. For hundreds of years, it was actually
illegal to kill or even shoo away this type of spider.

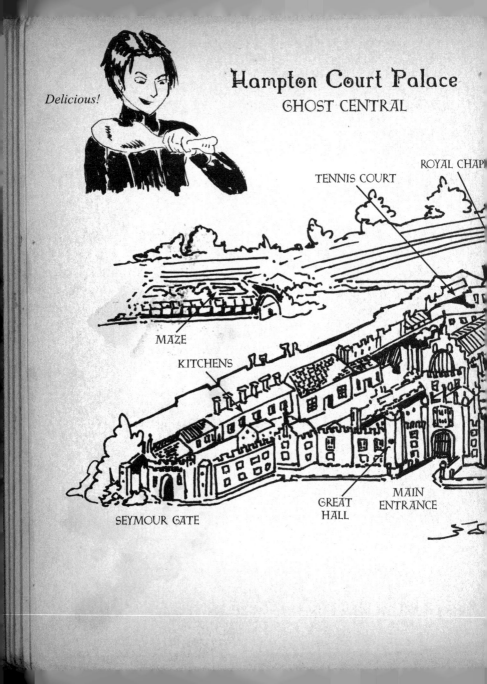

Delicious!

Hampton Court Palace
GHOST CENTRAL

ROYAL CHAP[EL]

TENNIS COURT

MAZE

KITCHENS

GREAT
HALL

MAIN
ENTRANCE

SEYMOUR GATE

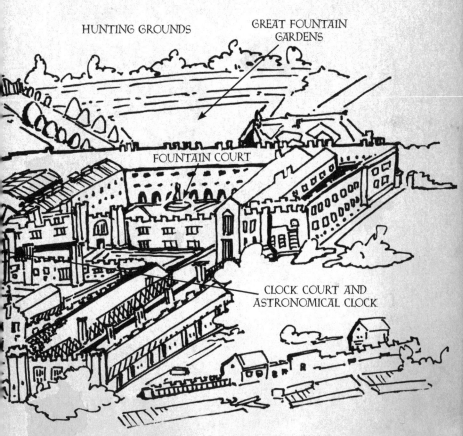

HUNTING GROUNDS   GREAT FOUNTAIN GARDENS

FOUNTAIN COURT

CLOCK COURT AND ASTRONOMICAL CLOCK

THAMES RIVER

It didn't take long for Henry VIII to become jealous of Wolsey's palace. The cardinal did the only thing he could do to keep his job as Lord Chancellor . . . and his head. He gave Hampton Court to Henry as a gift.

And here to help me talk more about Hampton Court . . . a ghost with auburn hair, a beautiful blue dress, and . . . carrying her own head? The forever doomed Queen Anne Boleyn. Queen Anne is often seen around the halls and gardens of the palace. People usually hear her crying and see her carrying her own head under one arm. Her troubles began in 1533, when she married King Henry VIII after he divorced his first wife, Queen Catherine of Aragon, of Spain.

Henry really loved Anne and hoped that she would one day give him a son to carry on the Tudor family's claim to the throne of England. Unfortunately, she had a daughter, Elizabeth. King Henry became furious and wanted to find a new wife who might bear him a son. He got rid of Anne in 1536 by having her found guilty of high treason against England (making evil plans against England). As punishment, her head was cut off with a sword.

I love a good party!

Good to see you again, Virgil.

SOCIETY PAGES PARTY REPORT
All the Popular People Were There!

"There were frequently great banquets . . .
the like of it was never given by Cleopatra; the
whole banqueting hall being decorated with
huge vases of gold and silver . . . Masquers
[were] disguised, all in one suit of fine green
satin, all over covered with cloth of gold . . . they
had danced . . . Then, they were served with a
supper of countless dishes of confections and
other delicacies . . . dancing commenced and
lasted till midnight and many hours later."

—*Hall's Chronicle*

Dinner at the Palace
THE GHOSTLY GUESTS ARE STILL FULL!

An important part of palace living was throwing grand parties with tons of fancy food. Let's visit the kitchen and find out what items were on a typical palace menu.

To our health and long life!

God save the king!

Meals were served in courses. Here are some of the foods found on a typical menu for a Tudor party:

Course One: Breads and Soups; Venison (deer); Mutton (sheep); Swan; Goose or Stork; Coney (rabbit); Carp; Eels; Salmon; Crabs and Lobster; Seals; Porpoises; Fruit

Course Two: Custard and Fritters; Jelly; Spiced Wine; Almond Cream; Pheasant; Heron; Peacocks; Sturgeon; Bream (fish); Lampreys (eel); Butter and Eggs; Seaweed Packed Salted Fish

Course Three: Pudding, Quinces

Fancy Roasted Peacock

1. Cut the skin off the peacock and set it aside. Don't damage the feathers!

2. Strip the meat off, remove the guts, and roast the meat on a spit until golden brown. Mix it with spices and other meats in the kitchen.

3. Stuff the cooked meat back into the original skin—careful with the feathers.

4. Arrange the bird on a serving tray. Spread out the tail feathers and place wood in the neck to hold up the head. Voila! A fancy dish for your party guests!

Five hundred years ago, there were no electric refrigerators to help preserve food, but they did have a cooling invention called an ice hut, cut into the ground and filled with huge blocks of ice. Palace cooks also used a lot of salt and sugar to keep food from spoiling, much as we sometimes add preservatives to our food today. Kids played a big role in the kitchen at Hampton Court, but it was no picnic.

Meat tastes better when a chef slowly turns it over a fire and keeps it moist with juice. This is called basting. Back then, kids standing just to the side of gigantic fireplaces were the ones who did the turning. Sometimes there were even special wheels for kids and dogs to walk in or on. In the winter, this wasn't so bad. But in the summer it could be sweltering. One advantage to this job was that the kids were always around food. It was a position that many wanted and only a lucky few got. Jobs at the palace varied—some were fantastic, others were less so.

Awesome and Awful Tudor Jobs

AWESOME PALACE JOBS

King—the ruler of a kingdom

Queen—the wife of the king and sometimes also a ruler in her own right

Knight—a soldier who rode a horse and protected the king

Bishop—very important priest in the church who controlled a lot of land and money

Yeager—a huntsman who helped the king on hunting expeditions

Yonker—a young knight

I love me!

AWFUL PALACE JOBS

Tumbrel boy—dung shoveler who cleaned up after all the animals

Tripe dresser—cleaned out cow and deer stomachs for the cooks to prepare barley and meat dishes that were cooked in stomach linings

Wart rubber—rubbed people's feet to make warts go away

Scoveler—climbed up into ovens and chimneys to clean out soot

Powder monkey—helped pack gunpowder into cannons

I wonder how far I can throw this?

Hellbrunn Water Palace— Amuse Me!

I'LL BET WE GET WET

Parties lasting weeks at a time were not the only way rulers entertained themselves. Hampton Court had everything a ruler could want in a palace. True, there were no video games, TV, Internet, or modern bathrooms. But the palace had theaters, beautiful gardens, amazing fountains, one of the first tennis courts, hunting grounds, and more.

And Hampton Court wasn't the only grand palace in the world. Many powerful rulers had a great sense of humor. They loved to use their money to buy the finest toys and mechanical devices that they could.

Royalty loved to show off their wealth and impress people by creating amazing gardens with mechanical fountains, beautiful works of art, and architectural feats. What's an architectural feat? Let's visit the amazing water gardens of Hellbrunn Palace, just outside Salzburg, Austria. It was designed and built from 1613 to about 1615 by Prince Archbishop Markus Sittikus von Hohenems. It rivaled any waterslide park built today—complete with practical jokes.

Hellbrunn, a wonderland of waterworks! Bring a towel.

Prince Archbishop Marcus Sittikus

DEER HEAD

Many of the statues and brassworks in Hellbrunn squirt water. Only Sittikus's friends knew to look for the laughing troll face that marked the trick squirting fountains.

DINING TABLE

Sittikus's dinner guests straddled the stone stools and would get squirted in the seat when the archbishop pressed a hidden button. One rule: Guests couldn't get up from the table before their host did.

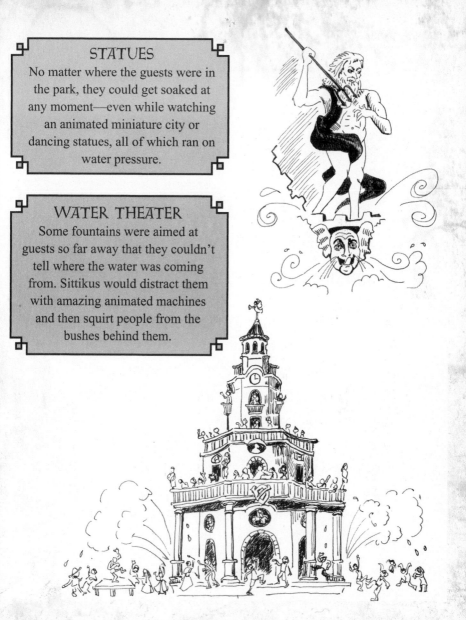

STATUES

No matter where the guests were in the park, they could get soaked at any moment—even while watching an animated miniature city or dancing statues, all of which ran on water pressure.

WATER THEATER

Some fountains were aimed at guests so far away that they couldn't tell where the water was coming from. Sittikus would distract them with amazing animated machines and then squirt people from the bushes behind them.

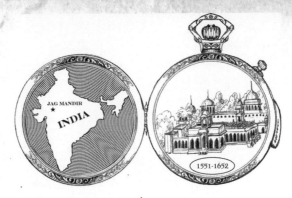

Jag Mandir Floating Palace

FAMILY ADVENTURES CARVED IN STONE

Oftentimes, kings used art, music, and theater to create elaborate stories about their family tree, tying themselves to myths of ancient rulers. This helped them legitimize their power. Royalty often addressed their subjects (the people they ruled over) from their palaces. Most subjects in a kingdom were very proud of the local palace, because many of them were involved in building or maintaining it. One of the most elaborate palaces ever built was Jag Mandir, in Udaipur, India.

The ruling families of this lake palace kept power by becoming not only kings but also the equivalent of gods in local mythologies. They didn't just put their stories on papyrus, clothes with embroidered symbols, and wood tablets; they wanted their stories to truly endure. They had them carved in stone, for everyone to see.

The palace was finished by Maharana Jagat Singh I (1628–1652). The elephants of Jag Mandir were built out of marble. In fact, the entire palace was made out of sandstone and marble. The life-sized elephants, which seemed to be standing on the water, were a symbol of the Singh family's amazing wealth and power.

The most famous story about Jag Mandir is about Singh's kindness toward the young Prince Khurram. The prince tried to overthrow the emperor, his father, but failed. He fled to Singh's kingdom, where he could live safely with his family. When his father died, Khurram finally became the emperor. This story is part of the Singh family history, which can still be found in the stone carvings of this beautiful palace.

Lose the attitude, prince.
You're lucky you survived.

4: The Graveyards

THE FINAL RESTING PLACE
THROUGH THE IRON GATES OF OBLIVION

Castles, dungeons, and palaces all served to help rulers define and defend land, keep control of their subjects, and show off power and wealth. These places helped rulers govern and negotiate with other rulers.

Similarly, graveyards were a huge part of the storytelling that helped to maintain the family power. Even in death, rulers liked to remind people of their place in history, and that was done through heraldry—symbols that represented powerful families.

Heraldry and
the Graveyard

CARVING FAMILY HISTORY IN STONE

Originally, a herald's job was to make announcements to his master's subjects. Heralds walked through town yelling information that the king wanted people to know, or announcing the presence of the king. They wore the symbols of their master's household on their clothes so that the subjects would know which royal family they represented. These were called heraldic symbols. The symbols were important for everyday news and information, but they were even more important in battle. Knights and soldiers could spot the symbols from a distance and tell the difference between the good guys and the bad guys. Over time, these symbols became an important part of identifying a royal or wealthy family in all areas of life, not just during battles.

Heraldic Symbols

The names used to describe the basic shield simply told people how the pattern of color was laid out on the surface of the shield:

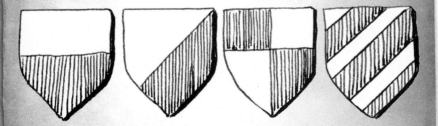

Per Fess A shield divided in half horizontally, with each half a different color

Per Bend Sinister A shield divided in half diagonally by a line going up to the left shoulder of the person carrying it (*sinister* originally meant "left" or "left-handed")

Quarterly A shield divided into four parts by a horizontal and a vertical line

Bendy Sinister Multiple colored stripes going up to the left

Once patterns and colors for a family were established, they were applied to all of the heraldic symbols, whether metal, cloth, or stone. Heraldic symbols came at a very high cost! In order to raise money for war efforts, several kings forced other nobility to create and register their heraldry with an official royal office. This fee became a way to tax the wealthiest people in the kingdom. Families concerned with losing their status at the king's court paid whether they liked it or not.

There are clues everywhere if you just know where to look.

Monuments and Burial

Heraldic symbols contain a lot of information. Families showed their heraldic symbols when they buried their dead. And what better way to indicate that the dead were still watching over the kingdom than with a monument or shrine?

✦ They identify the family of the deceased.

✦ They talk about famous conquests and battles that the family fought in.

✦ They show where a person was from and what type of crop or livestock the family produced.

✦ They tell whether or not a person was married and to which family.

✦ They reveal a person's political alliances.

✦ They list what religion, philosophy, career, and interests the person may have had.

The Secret Code of Heraldic Symbols

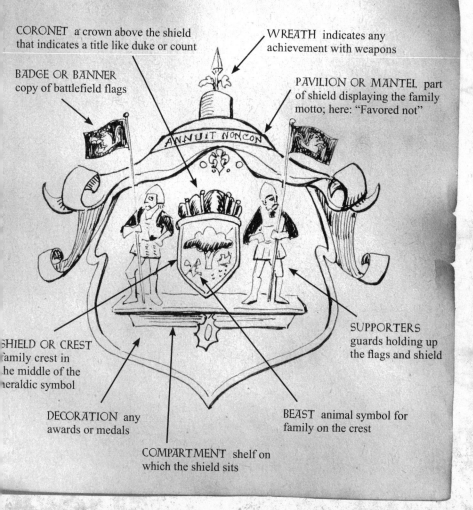

CORONET a crown above the shield that indicates a title like duke or count

WREATH indicates any achievement with weapons

BADGE OR BANNER copy of battlefield flags

PAVILION OR MANTEL part of shield displaying the family motto; here: "Favored not"

ANNUIT NONCON

SHIELD OR CREST family crest in the middle of the heraldic symbol

SUPPORTERS guards holding up the flags and shield

DECORATION any awards or medals

BEAST animal symbol for family on the crest

COMPARTMENT shelf on which the shield sits

What Goes into a Monument?

STONE-COLD DEAD...LIVES CARVED IN MARBLE

+ Monuments were big and expensive. Often they were created while the ruler was still alive.

+ Statues made the ruler look as good as possible. Usually the ruler was depicted as a strong, brave, wise, and heroic leader.

+ Plaques carved in stone told stories about how wonderful the ruler was.

+ The ruler was represented as a living person, as if he were relaxing or taking a long nap.

+ Monuments reminded people that a ruler's family was in power.

You try holding this pose for 500 years!

Royal family members were given a lesser burial place than the king, but it was still pretty good. Rulers also gave space to famous people who came from their kingdom, such as scholars, artists, architects, and religious figures. Where were all these great people buried? In the floor. The floor space was usually in a part of a chapel or church that was considered sacred. But it was still the floor and well below the giant, towering monuments erected by the rulers.

Peasants did not have it so lucky. The vast majority of them were buried in mass graves in churchyards, without headstones or markers. Wealthier townsfolk and city leaders like mayors and sheriffs almost always managed to secure a marker, headstone, or monument to their death and family name in their local churches and guild halls.

If you were famous,
you could be stuck
in the wall.

YOUR
NAME
HERE

The floor? Well, at
least it's inside....

Home, Haunted Home

Whether they were royal families, town mayors, or peasants in a field, all these people ended up equally dead and gone—ready for a Ghostorian, like me, to raise them for a friendly chat whenever I want to know a little more about their lives and their ancient worlds.

Until next time, I, Virgil, your humble Ghostorian, remind you that when you feel that shiver down your spine, or you're in a room that suddenly, and for no reason, gets a little too cold and dark—don't shrink in fear. Instead, call out a friendly hello to whoever might be haunting you—you never know what you can learn.

Haunted Histories Timeline

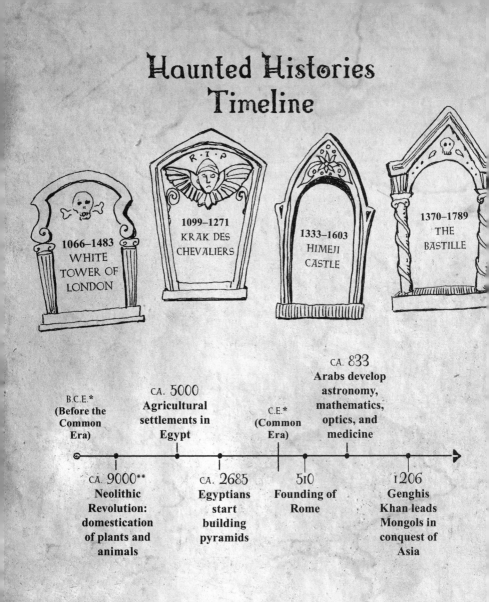

1066–1483 WHITE TOWER OF LONDON

1099–1271 KRAK DES CHEVALIERS

1333–1603 HIMEJI CASTLE

1370–1789 THE BASTILLE

B.C.E.*
(Before the Common Era)

CA. 5000
Agricultural settlements in Egypt

C.E.*
(Common Era)

CA. 833
Arabs develop astronomy, mathematics, optics, and medicine

CA. 9000**
Neolithic Revolution: domestication of plants and animals

CA. 2685
Egyptians start building pyramids

510
Founding of Rome

1206
Genghis Khan leads Mongols in conquest of Asia

1514–1838
HAMPTON
COURT
PALACE

1613–1615
HELLBRUNN
WATER
PALACE

1605–1627
JAG
MANDIR
FLOATING
PALACE

R.I.P

1854–1886
CASTLE
NEU-
SCHWAN-
STEIN

1348
**Black Death
hits Europe**

1776
**Declaration of
Independence
signed by the
13 colonies**

1973
**First working
cell phone
invented**

1325
**Aztecs at
their height
in Mexico**

1653
**Taj Mahal
built in India**

1848
**Gold
discovered in
California**

2010
**The first
iPad**

* In modern world history, B.C.E. and C.E. replace B.C. (Before Christ)
and A.D. (Anno Domini) for the historical timeline.

** CA. means "circa" or "about the time."

Hampt
Court
Palace
Englan

White
Tower of
London,
England

The
Bastille,
France

N

W   E

S

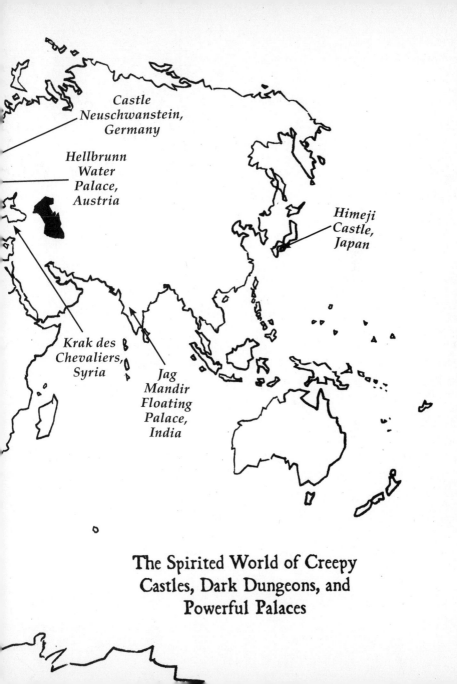

Castle
Neuschwanstein,
Germany

Hellbrunn
Water
Palace,
Austria

Himeji
Castle,
Japan

Krak des
Chevaliers,
Syria

Jag
Mandir
Floating
Palace,
India

The Spirited World of Creepy
Castles, Dark Dungeons, and
Powerful Palaces

Resources

Books

Aries, Philippe. *Centuries of Childhood: A Social History of Family Life.* Translated by Robert Baldick. New York: Vintage, 1965.

Gies, Joseph, and Francis Gies. *Life in a Medieval Castle.* New York: HarperCollins, 1981.

Nicholson, Helen. *Medieval Warfare: Theory and Practice of War in Europe, 300–1500.* New York: Palgrave Macmillan, 2004.

Slater, Stephen. *The Complete Book of Heraldry: An International History of Heraldry and Its Contemporary Uses.* London: Hermes House, 2003.

Websites

British Museum. http://www.britishmuseum.org.

National Archives of the United Kingdom. http://www.nationalarchives.gov.uk.

United States Library of Congress. http://www.loc.gov/index.html.

Index

Allures (walkways), 16
Amalasuntha, Queen of Goths, 46
Anne Boleyn, Queen of England, 93, 95, 100–101
Anne of Cleves, Queen of England, 93
Arrow loops, 31
Arthur Tudor, Prince of Wales, 94
Arundel, Philip Howard, Earl of, 65

Baibars, Sultan, 28–29, 41–42
Baileys, 16
Banquets and grand parties, 96, 102–7
  inviting enemies to, 89
Barbicans, 16

Bastille (Paris), 51, 72–73, 130, 132
Basting meat, 106
Bathrooms, 36
Battering rams, 43
Battlements, 16
Battles, 10
  attacking and defending castles in, 41–44
  castle design and, 12–13, 16–17, 19–22, 27–28, 30–31
  heraldic symbols in, 119
  revolting jobs for kids in, 45
Bavaria, Castle Neuschwanstein in, 51, 66–71, 131, 132
Beheadings, 93, 95, 100–101
Bishops, 108
Bones of animals, crushing, 83

Burials. *See* Graveyards
Burnings at the stake, 59, 61

Cardinal Spider (*Tegenaria
      parietina*), 97
Castle Berg (Bavaria), 70, 71
Castles, 9–49
   attacking and defending,
      41–44
   building, 12–13
   Himeji (Japan), 9, 18–23,
      130, 133
   insides of, 12, 35–38, 92
   Krak des Chevaliers (Syria),
      9, 27–31, 41–42, 130, 133
   Neuschwanstein (Bavaria),
      51, 66–71, 131, 132
   painted to look like stone,
      13, 15
   parts of, 16–17
   prisoners held in, 51–52.
      See also Dungeons and
      jails
   purposes of, 24–26, 33–34,
      48, 118
   White Tower (keep of Tower
      of London), 9, 33–40, 130,
      132
Catapult machines, 44
Catherine Howard, Queen of
   England, 93

Catherine of Aragon, Queen of
   England, 93, 94, 95,
   100–101
Catherine Park, Queen of
   England, 93
Cells, in prisons, 60, 62–63
City gate buildings, 51–52
Coins, with kings' portraits,
   50
Coronets, 123
Court officials, 25
Courtyards, of castles, 16
Craftsmen, 11, 25
Crimes and their punishments,
   74–75
Crusades, 27, 52–53
Curtain walls, 16

Death penalty, 59
Debtors, 56, 60, 73, 74
Deer heads, squirting, 112
Dickens, Charles, 58, 88
Digging and refilling holes,
   82, 85
Dining tables, squirting,
   112
Dodson, J. D., 85
Draper, Hugh, 63, 65
Drawbridges, 16
"Dungeon," origin of word,
   52

Dungeons and jails, 49, 51–89,
    118
    Bastille (Paris), 51, 72–73,
        130, 132
    built underground rather than
        in towers, 52–53
    in Castle Neuschwanstein
        (Bavaria), 51, 66–71, 131,
        132
    costs of being put in, 56–57,
        59
    kids in, 81–87
    Newgate Prison (London), 51,
        56–61
    organization of, 59–61
    rogues gallery of, 54–55
    torture in, 53, 62, 76–77
    see also Workhouses

Edward V, King of England,
    39–40
Edward VI, King of England, 95
Elephants, of Jag Mandir, 116
Elizabeth I, Queen of England,
    64, 95, 101
Embrasures, 31
Emperors, 11, 25
Enemies:
    hurling insults at, 45, 47
    parties for, 89
    see also Wars

Executioners, 55
Executions, 59
    burnings at the stake, 59, 61
    in Henry VIII's reign, 93, 95,
        100–101

Families, heraldic symbols and,
    118–24
Family mottoes, 123
Family tree, carved in stone at
    Jag Mandir, 114–15
Farmers, 11, 25
Feudal systems:
    in Europe (great chain of
        being), 10–11
    in Japan, 24, 25
Fitz Osbourne, Earl William,
    34
Floor spaces, burial in, 126,
    127
Food, 36
    Fancy Roasted Peacock
        recipe, 105
    gruel, 87, 88
    keeping from spoiling, 106
    roasting meat, 106–7
    at Tudor banquets and grand
        parties, 102–7
Fountains, at Hellbrunn Water
    Palace, 111–13
French Revolution, 73

Gaolers (jailers), 55
Garderobes, 36
Gatehouses, 17
Gates, of castles, 31
Germ warfare, 43
Gibbets, 13, 14, 78
Goths (Ostrogoths), 46–47
Graveyards, 118–27
    city leaders' burials in, 126
    famous people's burials in,
        126
    heraldic symbols in, 118–24
    monuments for rulers in,
        124–25, 126
    peasants' burials in, 126
    royal family members' burials
        in, 126
    wealthier townsfolk's burials
        in, 126
Great chain of being, 10–11
Gruel, 87, 88
Guards, 55

Hamlet (Shakespeare), 7
Hampton Court Palace (just
        outside London, England),
        90, 92–109, 131, 132
    Anne Boleyn's ghost in,
        100–101
    banquets and grand parties at,
        96, 102–7

layout of, 98–99
    recreational facilities at, 110
Heads, placed on spikes as
        warning, 13
Hellbrunn Water Palace (just
        outside Salzburg, Austria),
        90, 110–13, 131, 132
Henry VII, King of England,
        94
Henry VIII, King of England,
        93–95, 96, 100–101
Heraldic symbols, 118–24
    information contained in,
        122
    patterns of color on surface
        of, 129
    secret code of, 123
Himeji Castle (Japan), 9, 18–23,
        130, 133
    building of, 19–22
    defenses of, 20–21, 22
    ghost at, 22–23
Hundred Years' War, 72

Ikeda Terumasa, 19–22
Impressment, 79
Insults hurled at enemies, 45,
        47
Iron maiden (torture device),
        77
Isolation, as torture, 80

Jagat Singh I, Maharana, 116–17
Jag Mandir Floating Palace
(Udaipur, India), 90,
114–17, 131, 133
Jailers (gaolers), 55
Jails. *See* Dungeons and jails
Jane Grey, Queen of England, 65
Jane Seymour, Queen of
England, 93, 95
Japan, 18–26
feudal system in, 24, 25
Himeji Castle in, 9, 18–23,
130, 133
Kabuki theater in, 23–24
Judges, 54

Kabuki theater, 23–24
Keeps (castle buildings), 17, 40
see also White Tower
Khurram, Mughal Prince (future
Shah Jahan), 117
Kings, 11, 108
castles built by, 10, 12–13
Knights, 11, 46, 108, 119
Hospitallers, 27–29
Knowing too much of king's
business, 75
Krak des Chevaliers (Syria), 9,
27–31, 130, 133
defenses of, 30–31
living through siege of, 41–42

Leicester, Robert Dudley, Earl
of, 64
Lettres de cachet, 73
London, England:
Newgate Prison in, 51,
56–61
see also Hampton Court
Palace; Tower of London;
White Tower
Lords, 11, 46
castles built by, 10, 12–13
Louis XIV, King of France, 50
Ludwig II, King of Bavaria,
66–71

Machicolations, 30
Mamluk, 28–29, 41–42
Mangonels, 43
Markus Sittikus von Hohenems,
Prince Archbishop, 111
Mary I, Queen of England, 95
Meat, roasting, 106–7
Menus, for Tudor parties, 103–5
Merchants, 11, 25
Merlons, 31
Milling grain, 83
Minister's chair (torture device),
78
Moats, 12, 17, 22, 30, 36
Monuments, for burial of rulers,
124–25, 126

Needlework, 84, 85
Neuschwanstein dungeon
    (Bavaria), 51, 66–71, 131,
    132
Newgate Prison (London), 51,
    56–61

Oakum, 82, 85
Okiku, 22–23
Ostrogoths (Goths), 46–47
Otto, King of Bavaria, 70–71

Palaces, 90–117
    awesome jobs in, 108
    awful jobs in, 109
    banquets and grand parties at,
        96, 102–7
    Hellbrunn Water Palace
        (just outside Salzburg,
        Austria), 90, 110–13, 131,
        132
    Jag Mandir Floating Palace
        (Udaipur, India), 90,
        114–17, 131, 133
    purposes of, 90–93, 115,
        118
    toys and mechanical devices
        in, 110–13
    see also Hampton Court
        Palace
Parapets, 17

Paris, France, Bastille in, 51,
    72–73, 130, 132
Parties. See Banquets and grand
    parties
Peacock, Fancy Roasted, 105
Peasants, 10, 11, 25, 126
Poor people:
    punishment of, 74
    see also Debtors
Popes, 11
Portcullises, 17
Posterns, 17
Powder monkeys, 109
Prisons. See Dungeons and
    jails
Procopius, 46
Punishment:
    for various crimes, 74–75
    see also Dungeons and jails;
        Executions

Queens, 11, 108

Rack (torture device), 76
Raleigh, Sir Walter, 64
Revolutionaries, 75
Rich and powerful, punishment
    of, 75
Richard, Duke of York, 39–40
Richard III, King of England,
    39–40, 94

Richelieu, Cardinal, 72
Romans, 56

Salzburg, Austria, Hellbrunn
    Water Palace just outside,
    90, 110–13, 131, 132
Samurai, 19, 25
Scavenger's daughter (torture
    device), 79
Schools, Goths' views on,
    46–47
Scold's bride (torture device), 80
Scovelers, 109
Servants, 36, 59, 62
Shackles, 77
Shakespeare, William, 6, 7
Sheriffs, 54
Shoguns and shogunates, 18, 25
Siege towers, 42, 43
Singh family, Jag Mandir and,
    116–17
Sissies, 45, 47
Slingshots, 44
Smooching the queen, 75
Springalds, 42, 44
Spying, 75
Statues:
    on rulers' burial monuments,
        125
    squirting, at Hellbrunn Water
        Palace, 113

Stealing, 74
Stone:
    breaking and moving,
        83, 85
    building with, 12, 26
    family tree carved in,
        at Jag Mandir,
        114–15
    messages and graffiti
        scratched on, by prisoners,
        63–65
    wood castles painted to look
        like, 13, 15
Syria, Krak des Chevaliers in,
    9, 27–31, 41–42, 130,
    133

Talking ill of the king, 74
Taxes, heraldic symbols and,
    121
Telling bad jokes, 74
Tennis courts, 110
Thumbscrews, 76
Tokugawa shogunate, 19–22
Torture, 53, 62, 76–77
Tower of London (England):
    keep of. See White Tower
    messages and graffiti carved
        on, by famous prisoners,
        63–65
    prison in, 51, 59, 62–65

Towers, of castles, 17, 30
Toys and mechanical devices, at
    Hellbrunn Water Palace,
    110–13
Trebuchets, 43
Trials, 56–57
Tripe dressers, 109
Tumbrel boys, 109
Turnkey rooms, 60

Udaipur, India, Jag Mandir
    Floating Palace in, 90,
    114–17, 131, 133

Wagner, Richard, 68
Wards, in prisons, 60
Warlords, 25
Wars. *See* Battles
Wart rubbers, 109
Washing and scrubbing, 84, 85
Water gardens, of Hellbrunn
    Palace, 110–13

White Tower (keep of Tower of
    London, England), 9,
    33–40, 130, 132
    ghosts in, 39–40
    inside of, 35–38
William I (William the
    Conqueror), King of
    England, 33–35
Wolsey, Cardinal Thomas,
    96–100
Wood, cutting and stacking, 84,
    85
Workhouses, 81–89
    daily activities for kids in,
    82–85
    fighting in, 86
    gruel in, 87, 88

Yeagers, 108
Yonkers, 108
Yuurei (Japanese female ghost),
    22

About the Authors

J. H. EVERETT holds a Ph.D. in medieval history from the University of California, Irvine. He enjoys writing and drawing stories about all the creepy places that he visits. He lives in southern California. [jheverett.com]

MARILYN SCOTT-WATERS likes collecting old books, sketching in art museums, and making things out of paper. She is the creator of *The Toymaker's Christmas: Paper Toys You Can Make Yourself* and *The Toymaker's Workshop: Paper Toys You Can Make Yourself*. She lives in southern California. [thetoymaker.com]